# ADVENTURING

# WITH

# GOD

*Following*
—— *in the* ——
*Apostles' Footsteps*

*From the Bible-Teaching Ministry of*

## Charles R. Swindoll

INSIGHT *for* LIVING

*Insight for Living*'s Bible teacher, Chuck Swindoll, has devoted his life to the clear, practical application of God's Word and His grace. A pastor at heart, Chuck has served as senior pastor to congregations in Texas, Massachusetts, and California. He currently leads Stonebriar Community Church in Frisco, Texas, but Chuck's listening audience extends far beyond a local church body. As a leading program in Christian broadcasting, *Insight for Living* airs in major Christian radio markets, through more than 2,100 outlets worldwide, in 16 languages, and to a growing webcast audience. Chuck's extensive writing ministry has also served the body of Christ worldwide, and his leadership as president and now chancellor of Dallas Theological Seminary has helped prepare and equip a new generation for ministry. Chuck and Cynthia, his partner in life and ministry, have four grown children and ten grandchildren.

Based on the outlines, charts, and transcripts of Charles R. Swindoll's sermons, the study guide text was developed and written by the creative ministries department of Insight for Living.

**Editor in Chief:**
Cynthia Swindoll

**Study Guide Writer:**
Marla Alupoaicei

**Editor:**
Amy LaFuria

**Typesetter:**
Bob Haskins

**Rights and Permissions:**
The Meredith Agency

Unless otherwise identified, all Scripture references are from the New American Standard Bible © The Lockman Foundation 1960, 1962, 1963, 1968, 1971, 1972, 1973, 1975, 1977, 1995. Used by permission. Scripture taken from the Holy Bible, New International Version, copyright © 1973, 1978, 1984 by the International Bible Society, used by permission of Zondervan Bible Publishers [NIV].

An effort has been made to locate sources and obtain permission where necessary for the quotations used in this book. In the event of any unintentional omission, a modification will gladly be incorporated in future printings.

ISBN 1-57972-513-9
Cover design: Alex Pasieka
Cover image: Mount Baker (PhotoDisc Inc.: Nature, Wildlife and the Environment, vol. 6, Copyright © 1993)
Printed in the United States of America

# CONTENTS

# INTRODUCTION

Have you ever thought of your Christian life as an adventure of extraordinary proportions? If not, come with us on an awe-inspiring journey with Jesus' disciples, where we'll experience one miraculous encounter after another.

Christ's faithful followers squeezed as much as they could out of life. Each of them awoke in the morning wondering, *God, what incredible adventures do You have in store for me today?* And they never lacked for surprises! In fact, the book titled The Acts of the Apostles contains so much intrigue that it could have been called The Adventures of the Apostles.

These believers learned that a life of adventure requires passion, enthusiasm, and a willingness to take risks. The setbacks they endured only fueled the flame in their hearts, firing up their determination to take the Gospel to the world. They forged ahead with conviction, knowing that God's blessings far outweighed life's difficulties.

As we explore the remarkable adventures that God bestowed on the apostles, another term comes to mind—*serendipity*. When something beautiful and unexpected breaks the monotony of our daily routines, we experience God's serendipity in all its fullness. Once we learn to appreciate good gifts and delightful surprises from the hand of God, we'll start to consider our adventures serendipities—unexpected blessings that we encounter along life's journey.

*Charles R. Swindoll*

Charles R. Swindoll

# PUTTING TRUTH
# INTO ACTION

Knowledge apart from application falls short of God's desire for His children. He wants us to apply what we learn so that we will change and grow. This Bible study guide was prepared with these goals in mind. As you go through the following pages, we hope your desire to discover biblical truth will grow as your understanding of God's Word increases and that you will be encouraged to apply what you've learned.

To assist you in your study, we've included a section called Living Insights at the end of each lesson. These exercises will challenge you to study further and to think of specific ways to put your discoveries into action.

There are many ways to use this guide—in personal devotions, group studies, discussions with friends and family, and Sunday school classes. And, of course, it's an ideal study aid when you're listening to its corresponding *Insight for Living* radio series.

To benefit most from this Bible study guide, we encourage you to consider it a spiritual journal. That's why we've included space in the Living Insights for recording your thoughts and discoveries. We hope you'll return to those sections often for review and encouragement as you continue to grow in your walk with Christ.

Insight for Living

# ADVENTURING
## WITH
# GOD

## Chapter 1

# REACHING OUR WORLD
### Acts 1:1–11

Jim Elliot once wrote in his journal, "Wherever you are, be all there. Live to the hilt every situation you believe to be the will of God."[1]

Completely sold out to God, this young man impressed everyone he met with his humble spirit, his radical love for Christ, and his consuming passion for the lost. After he graduated from Wheaton College in 1949, Elliot committed his life to sharing the Gospel with several unreached Indian tribes in Ecuador. He ministered successfully there for several years with his wife, Elisabeth. But when Jim and four friends tried to establish contact with the reclusive Auca Indian tribe, they were suddenly and brutally murdered by fierce Auca warriors.

In His own way, God used this seemingly tragic event for His glory. The news media, intrigued by Elliot's faith, courage, and adventurous spirit, spread his poignant story to millions of people throughout the world. *LIFE* magazine featured a ten-page article on the life and mission of Elliot and the four other young men. As a result, Jim Elliot is now known as one of the greatest missionary-martyrs of our time.

And that's not the end of the story! Incredibly, Jim Elliot's desire to share Christ with unreached Indian tribes lived on through his courageous wife, Elisabeth. She eventually returned to Ecuador to minister to the Auca Indians—the very people who had killed her husband. She shared the message of God's love with the Aucas and saw many come to faith in Christ.

---

1. "The Seeking Life," accessed on September 13, 2002, available at http://www.in-touch.org/myintouch/mighty/portraits/jim_elliot_213678.html.

# The Adventures of the Apostles

Like the Elliots, Jesus' disciples knew what it meant to "live to the hilt." As they encountered one adventure after another, they learned how to be "all there," no matter what the cost. In fact, the Bible book we now know as The Acts of the Apostles contains so much drama and intrigue that it could have been called The Adventures of the Apostles!

Merriam-Webster's defines *adventure* as "an undertaking usually involving danger and unknown risks; the encountering of risks; an exciting or remarkable experience; or an enterprise involving financial risk."[2] Notice that the word "risk" appears again and again! The apostles braved it all to follow God's call, taking the life-changing Gospel message to the world.

As we explore the remarkable experiences and surprise blessings that God bestowed on the apostles, another term comes to mind. Ever heard the word *serendipity*? It means "the faculty or phenomenon of finding valuable or agreeable things not sought for."[3] Think of it as *"seren-dip-ity*—the *dip* of the *serene* into the common responsibilities of life. Serendipity occurs when something beautiful breaks into the monotonous and the mundane. A serendipitous life is marked by 'surprisability' and spontaneity. When we lose our capacity for either, we settle into life's ruts."[4] But if we expect the best from God, the sky's the limit! So consider your adventures *serendipities*—unexpected blessings that occur along life's journey.

Serendipities require vision and courage, and they also bring with them a measure of uncertainty. But that's what makes life interesting! Oswald Chambers wrote,

> "Certainty is the mark of the commonsense life— gracious uncertainty is the mark of the spiritual life. To be certain of God means that we are uncertain in all our ways, not knowing what tomorrow may bring."[5]

2. *Merriam-Webster's Collegiate Dictionary*, 10th ed., see "adventure."

3. *Merriam-Webster's Collegiate Dictionary*, 10th ed., see "serendipity."

4. Charles R. Swindoll, from the daily devotional entitled "Expecting the Unexpected," in *The Finishing Touch: Becoming God's Masterpiece* (Dallas, Tex.: Word Publishing, 1994), p. 130.

5. Oswald Chambers, *My Utmost for His Highest*, "Gracious Uncertainty," accessed October 4, 2002, available at www.gospel.com.net/rbc/utmost-devo/search, April 29 entry.

When we choose to let "gracious uncertainty" and God's serendipity define our faith, we experience His blessing to the fullest. As we become more mature believers, we learn to relinquish control and trust Him. Such a radical faith requires personal risk and an adventurous spirit. It means denying ourselves, taking up our crosses, and following Christ daily. Oswald Chambers continued, "This [uncertainty] is generally expressed with a sigh of sadness but it should be an expression of breathless expectation."[6]

How often do we face the day with "breathless expectation"? Instead, we usually groan when the alarm goes off and hit the snooze button to gain a few more minutes of sleep. But preparing for a life of adventure means placing our faith in God, getting our act together, and making a difference. The Lord had this in mind when he transformed eleven frightened disciples into brave, confident adventurers who spread the Gospel throughout the entire known world.

## The Marks of an Adventurer

What attributes did these adventurous apostles possess? They followed God's call and searched out new ways to share the Gospel. They ministered to others, even in the face of extreme danger. They were willing to accept the risks that came with the pursuit of God's kingdom. And it was in the midst of these eleven men that Jesus made a promise that revolutionized the world: "I will build my church" (Matt. 16:18). At that time, He hadn't yet started the construction project. But the apostles realized that they were experiencing the birth of something new and incredible.

The physician Luke, sometimes called "Doctor Luke," wrote the book of Acts. Inspired by the Holy Spirit, Luke created a profound, historically accurate, and gripping narrative about the early church. He exhibited an excellent command of the Greek language, peppering his writings with technical terms. Luke began the book of Acts this way:

> The first account I composed, Theophilus, about
> all that Jesus began to do and teach . . . (v. 1)

Here, Luke referred to a "first account" that he had previously written. What was this first account? The Gospel According to Luke.

---

6. Chambers, My Utmost for His Highest, "Gracious Uncertainty."

The purpose of Luke's gospel had been to record in detail Jesus' words and deeds so that every generation of Christians could read them. What happened at the end of this first account? Luke reminded us in verses 2–3 of Acts 1:

> . . . until the day when He was taken up to heaven, after He had by the Holy Spirit given orders to the apostles whom He had chosen. To these He also presented Himself alive after His suffering, by many convincing proofs, appearing to them over a period of forty days and speaking of the things concerning the kingdom of God. (vv. 2–3)

Notice the vital facts that Luke emphasized in these verses. First, Christ had risen from the dead and had appeared to the apostles and many others, offering physical proof of His bodily resurrection. And then He had ministered to the people, teaching them concerning the kingdom of God.

Before He ascended, Jesus gave the disciples a final command:

> Gathering them together, He commanded them not to leave Jerusalem, but to wait for what the Father had promised, "Which," He said, "you heard of from Me . . ." (v. 4)

What were the apostles to wait for? The outpouring of the Holy Spirit of God. Jesus' apostles, friends, and followers were not going to be left to face life alone. Jesus reminded them that the Father had promised to send them a Guide and a Comforter. The power of the Spirit would soon flow, filling these men with strength and giving them a vision for how God would use them to impact their world.

## Four Contrasts Regarding the Holy Spirit

Jesus assured His disciples that *the Holy Spirit was not a symbol, but a reality*. He promised them:

> ". . . for John baptized with water, but you will be baptized with the Holy Spirit not many days from now." (v. 5)

"Baptized with the Holy Spirit"? The disciples probably wondered what exactly this meant, since no one had ever before received the permanent indwelling of the Spirit of God. But they would soon witness the presence of the third member of the Trinity in all His glory. They were about to receive the power, discernment, and wisdom to take on adventures they had never before imagined.

The apostles felt great excitement, but they were also confused. They asked Jesus a question to try to figure out what He meant by His statement:

> So when they had come together, they were ask-
> ing Him, saying, "Lord, is it at this time You are
> restoring the kingdom to Israel?" (v. 6)

From their question, it's clear that the apostles misunderstood Jesus' statement regarding the sending of the Holy Spirit. They had trouble thinking past the "here and now" to the "then and there" part of Jesus' message, assuming that the sending of the Holy Spirit meant that Jesus' kingdom on earth was about to begin. The verb "restore" shows that they expected a political, territorial kingdom. The noun "Israel" indicates that they expected a national kingdom. And the adverbial clause "at this time" shows that they thought the kingdom's establishment was imminent.[7]

Jesus, recognizing their confusion, clarified the issue for the apostles. He showed them that *the sending of the Holy Spirit was not a program but a power*. He corrected their mistaken notions regarding the kingdom's nature, extent, and arrival:

> He said to them, "It is not for you to know times or
> epochs which the Father has fixed by His own au-
> thority; but you will receive power when the Holy
> Spirit has come upon you; and you shall be My
> witnesses both in Jerusalem, and in all Judea and
> Samaria, and even to the remotest part of the earth."
> (Acts 1:7–8)

Jesus informed the apostles that *they were not just promoters; they were witnesses*. In place of their confusion, fearfulness, and misguided notions about the kingdom, Jesus' apostles would receive knowl-edge, courage, wisdom, and power through the outpouring of the Holy Spirit. And, to ensure that His kingdom work continued on earth, what did Jesus do after assuring the apostles that they would

---

7. John Stott, *The Spirit, the Church, and the World: The Message of Acts* (Downers Grove, Ill.: InterVarsity Press, 1992), p. 40.

soon receive the Spirit? That's right—He left!

> And after He had said these things, He was lifted up while they were looking on, and a cloud received Him out of their sight. And as they were gazing intently into the sky while he was going, behold, two men in white clothing stood beside them. They also said, "Men of Galilee, why do you stand looking into the sky? This Jesus, who has been taken up from you into heaven, will come in just the same way as you have watched Him go into heaven." (vv. 9–11)

Jesus ascended to heaven. His work on earth was accomplished. He left the apostles with a vision for their role in the furthering of the kingdom of God. And *this kingdom was not limited; it was universal.* The apostles were called to take the Gospel to all people— even to the ends of the earth.

The awestruck apostles continued to look up into the sky as Jesus ascended. The looks on their faces must have reflected the question of their hearts—"Lord, You're leaving? What do we do now?" But then two angels appeared, reminding the disciples that Jesus would someday return in the same way He had gone. Their essential message? "Stop looking up into the sky and get busy!"

Do you ever need to be reminded to "Stop looking around and get busy"? You live with the fervent hope of Jesus' return. You have the Holy Spirit of God to comfort and guide you. You've been given the Great Commission to take the Gospel to every creature. So seize your opportunity to live each day to the fullest, and be on the lookout for the special serendipities God may send your way. Ask God to make today an adventure that you'll never forget!

 ## *Living Insights*

Some aspects of God and His kingdom remain incomprehensible and mysterious to us. But we know this much: He delights in surprising us. He dots our pilgrimage from earth to heaven with incredible adventures and amazing serendipities. The Lord told the prophet Isaiah:

> See, I am doing a new thing!
> Now it springs up; do you not perceive it?

I am making a way in the desert
And streams in the wasteland. (Isa. 43:19 NIV)

What serendipities have occurred in your life in the past? What did you learn from them?

_____

_____

_____

_____

_____

What "new things" do you feel God wants to do in your life right now?

_____

_____

_____

_____

Is anything hindering your progress in these areas? If so, what?

_____

_____

_____

_____

Take some time now to pray about these hindrances in your life. Then list some steps you can take personally to overcome them. Also, list the name of one person you can ask to keep you accountable.

_____

_____

_____

_____

_____

_____

_____

_____

   Part of your adventure with God involves goal setting. What
are your goals for the next year (or even the next month)? How
do you hope to accomplish them?

_____

_____

_____

_____

_____

_____

_____

# BIRTHING THE CHURCH

*Acts 2:1–13; 37–47*

On November 19, 1997, Kenneth and Bobbi McCaughey of Carlisle, Iowa, became the proud parents of the world's only surviving set of septuplets.

Doctors had advised the McCaugheys early in the pregnancy that aborting some of the fetuses through a process called "selective reduction" would increase the chances of survival of the others. But the McCaugheys refused to do so on the basis of their strong faith in God. Along with thousands of friends, neighbors, and well-wishers, they prayed fervently for the septuplets' health and safety. And on that serendipitous November day, the McCaugheys were rewarded with seven healthy babies: Kenneth, Alexis, Natalie, Kelsey, Brandon, Nathanial, and Joel.[1]

Having seven children at one time would be difficult enough, but can you imagine experiencing three thousand new births? What an adventure! That's what happened on the day of Pentecost. A large gathering of people witnessed the incredible, supernatural power of the Holy Spirit and heard the life-changing Gospel message preached by Peter and the other apostles. As a result, over three thousand new believers came into the Christian faith that day.

## The Significance of Pentecost

Let's take a moment to explore the significance of the day of Pentecost for the Jewish community. In Greek, the word *Pentecost* literally means "fiftieth."[2] Pentecost, also called the Feast of Weeks, was a festival that the Jewish people celebrated on the fiftieth day after Passover. During this time, God's people expressed their thanksgiving to Him for the harvest.

---

1. "Septuplets 'a Miracle'" *The Gazette* (Cedar Rapids, Iowa), published online Nov. 20, 1997, available at http://www.gazetteonline.com/special/babies/seps001.htm, accessed on September 23, 2002.

2. William F. Arndt, F. Wilbur Gingrich, and Frederick W. Danker, eds., *A Greek-English Lexicon of the New Testament*, 2d ed. (Chicago, Ill.: The University of Chicago Press, 1979), p. 643.

Chapter 2 of the book of Acts begins on this day of Pentecost, with the apostles and a group of believers gathered in the Upper Room. Luke wrote in verse 1, "They were all together in one place." According to verse 15, about 120 people were gathered there for this annual celebration.

It's been said, "That's the last time the church was 'all together' while in one place!" Why? Because these believers experienced true unity in heart and spirit, unlike many churches today. The early church had no building, no pastor, no denominations, and no constitution. But they were united with common purposes: loving and serving the Lord Jesus Christ and caring for each other.

## The Sending of the Holy Spirit

In Acts 2:1–13, Luke recorded an extraordinary scene. The Holy Spirit swept through the Upper Room with the sound of a powerful wind, alighting on each person with tongues of flame:

> When the day of Pentecost had come, they were all together in one place. And suddenly there came from heaven a noise like a violent rushing wind, and it filled the whole house where they were sitting. And there appeared to them tongues as of fire distributing themselves, and they rested on each one of them. And they were all filled with the Holy Spirit and began to speak with other tongues, as the Spirit was giving them utterance. (vv. 1–4)

Talk about an adventure! Those who received the Holy Spirit in the Upper Room that day experienced three remarkable occurrences: they *heard* something, they *saw* something, and they *said* something.

### They Heard Something

Those gathered around heard "a noise like a violent rushing wind, and it filled the whole house where they were sitting" (v. 2). The sound of the Spirit being sent from heaven to earth filled their ears as God performed a new and extraordinary thing. These men must have realized that the "winds of change" were blowing as the Spirit swept into their midst. Their lives would never be the same again!

### They Saw Something

Not only did these men hear and feel the wind of the Spirit filling the Upper Room, they also saw "tongues as of fire distributing themselves, and they rested on each one of them" (v. 3). They experienced the power of God as the Holy Spirit manifested Himself in the forms of wind and fire.

Though believers no longer experience the presence of the Holy Spirit in the form of these elements, He is just as powerful and evident in our spiritual lives today as He was at the time of Pentecost.

### They Said Something

What was the result of the people hearing the wind of the Spirit and being anointed by flames of fire? They began to speak, proclaiming the Gospel and the mighty works of God. Verse 4 reads, "And they were all filled with the Holy Spirit and began to speak with other tongues, as the Spirit was giving them utterance."

God called them to action! In the same way, His Spirit empowers us to proclaim the Gospel to those around us. Are you sharing the love of God with others through your words and actions?

## The Working of the Holy Spirit

Let's read on to see what happened next:

> Now there were Jews living in Jerusalem, devout men from every nation under heaven. And when this sound occurred, the crowd came together, and were bewildered because each one of them was hearing them speak in his own language. (vv. 5–6)

As the apostles and other believers preached the Gospel, a large crowd gathered around. And, incredibly, each person heard the apostles speaking in his or her own language:

> They were amazed and astonished, saying, "Why, are not all these who are speaking Galileans? And how is it that we each hear them in our own language to which we were born? Parthians and Medes and Elamites, and residents of Mesopotamia, Judea and Cappadocia, Pontus and Asia, Phrygia and Pamphylia, Egypt and the districts of Libya around Cyrene, and visitors from Rome, both Jews and pros-

elytes, Cretans and Arabs—we hear them in our own tongues speaking of the mighty deeds of God." And they all continued in amazement and great perplexity, saying to one another, "What does this mean?" But others were mocking and saying, "They are full of sweet wine." (vv. 7–13)

What an extraordinary experience! Not only had the crowd seen a truly astonishing sight, but now they couldn't believe their ears! Each member of this crowd—Jews, Greeks, Medes, Egyptians—could hear the Gospel being spoken in his or her *own language*. Notice that these were not *unknown* tongues, but rather, the natural languages of the people.

## The Response of the Crowd

A few members of the crowd scoffed at all the hubbub, suggesting that the apostles were drunk (v. 13). But most of the people recognized what an astonishing supernatural event they were witnessing. Their hearts stirred within them, and they knew they had to respond:

> Now when they heard this, they were pierced to the heart, and said to Peter and the rest of the apostles, "Brethren, what shall we do?" Peter said to them, "Repent, and each of you be baptized in the name of Jesus Christ for the forgiveness of your sins; and you will receive the gift of the Holy Spirit. For the promise is for you and your children and for all who are far off, as many as the Lord our God will call to Himself." And with many other words he solemnly testified and kept on exhorting them, saying, "Be saved from this perverse generation!" (vv. 37–40)

After they had heard the Gospel, what was the next step for these men whose hearts had been "pierced" by the Holy Spirit?

> So then, those who had received his word were baptized; and that day there were added about three thousand souls. (v. 41)

Three thousand new "babies" had been born into God's family, and they wanted everyone around them to know about their new-found commitment. So they publicly proclaimed their faith in Jesus

Christ through baptism. They made this their first step of obedience to Christ.

## The Priorities of the Church

After being baptized, the first great task for these new members of the body of Christ was learning how to worship and fellowship together in a unified way. And they excelled at it!

> They were continually devoting themselves to the apostles' teaching and to fellowship, to the breaking of bread and to prayer. Everyone kept feeling a sense of awe; and many wonders and signs were taking place through the apostles. (vv. 42–43)

Verse 42 identifies four of the primary purposes of the early church: teaching, fellowship, breaking of bread, and prayer.

### Teaching

The backbone of a growing, healthy Christian is the constant intake of a balanced diet of spiritual nourishment. The new believers mentioned here gained knowledge and maturity as they sat under the apostles' teaching. They received a solid diet of healthy spiritual food. We can't stay strong without this spiritual sustenance. If there's no teaching, we're simply having a picnic, a potluck, or a party. Without solid instruction, we're a fellowship gathering, not a church!

### Fellowship

The Greek term for fellowship, *koinonia*, carries the idea of familiarity and sharing. *Koinonia* normally has one of two connotations: sharing something with someone or sharing *in* something with another person. These early believers blended their lives together with a sense of closeness, oneness, and harmony. Like them, we fellowship by sharing words of encouragement. We minister to others by offering our money and resources to those in need. We hold each other accountable by bringing reproofs and giving warnings when necessary. We offer confessions and admit our needs as we share in the joys, griefs, and common life experiences of others. Remember: we can't have teaching without fellowship. If we do, we're a school, not a church!

13

### Breaking of Bread

Early Christians carefully observed the ordinances of communion and baptism. The sacraments of the church were administered as a part of the worship service. Without the Lord's Table and without baptism, we lose important reminders of Christ's sacrifice. Without worship, communion, and baptism, we're a secular gathering, not a spiritual one.

### Prayer

Prayer stands as a vital element of the church. Like a lightning rod channeling an enormous power source, prayer connects us with the living God. It ushers us into God's awesome presence and serves as our stabilizing force, humbling us and reminding us of our position before God. Prayer offers us a relationship like no other—the opportunity to not only speak with, but to listen to the almighty God. It's the means by which we express our love and thankfulness to Him.

Three thousand new "babies" in Christ grew and matured in their faith by integrating these four elements into their worship experience. Not only did these Christians share the cornerstones of the faith, but they also shared their possessions in an incredibly self-sacrificing way:

> And all those who had believed were together and had all things in common; and they began selling their property and possessions and were sharing them with all, as anyone might have need. Day by day continuing with one mind in the temple, and breaking bread from house to house, they were taking their meals together with gladness and sincerity of heart, praising God and having favor with all the people. And the Lord was adding to their number day by day those who were being saved. (vv. 44–47)

What compassion, unity, and loving attitudes these early believers displayed toward one another! These verses remind us of how we are to live our lives as true followers of Christ. Not only are we called to be salt and light to the non-Christian world, but we're called to be kind and minister to the needs of those within the church body. We're expected to give sacrificially to them while praising God for the opportunity to serve.

Is your church body known for its self-sacrifice, thanksgiving, close fellowship, and sincerity of heart? If not, it's time to get back to the basics. As you continue to study the birth of the church and learn to follow the example of the first Christians, you can become for your church a model of dynamic and authentic faith.

 *Living Insights*

When those in the Upper Room experienced the giving of the Holy Spirit, they *heard* Him, they *saw* Him, and they *spoke* as they were moved by Him. Take some time now to consider the Spirit's role in your own life.

How do you hear God's voice in your life? In what ways have you experienced the Holy Spirit "speaking" to you in your spirit?

_____

_____

_____

_____

Has the Holy Spirit ever spoken to you through other people? If so, describe your experience below.

_____

_____

_____

_____

Have you ever felt the conviction of the Holy Spirit piercing your heart like the members of the crowd did in Acts 2? If so, what happened, and what was your response?

_____

_____

_____

_____

_____

Have you ever experienced a divine encounter—when you felt the Holy Spirit leading you to reach out to someone or to share the Gospel with him or her? If so, what happened?

_____

_____

_____

_____

Is the Lord leading you to share your faith with someone in your life right now? If so, who is it? How can you prepare yourself to speak with this person about spiritual matters?

_____

_____

_____

_____

## Chapter 3

# TOUCHING OTHERS' LIVES

### Acts 8:25–40

A uthor John Eldredge writes, "Life is not a problem to be solved; it is an adventure to be lived."[1] He continues,

> That's the nature of it and has been since the beginning when God set the dangerous stage for this high-stakes drama and called the whole wild enterprise *good*. He rigged the world in such a way that it only works when we embrace *risk* as the theme of our lives, which is to say, only when we live by faith. [We] just won't be happy until [we've] got adventure in [our] work, in [our] love, and in [our] spiritual lives.[2]

The apostles certainly had their share of adventure! After receiving the Holy Spirit in the Upper Room at Pentecost, they embarked on the journey of a lifetime. Empowered and emboldened by the Spirit, they preached the Gospel and performed extraordinary miracles, touching others' lives as they went. Let's take a look at how they effectively ministered to others so we can discover some positive principles to use in our own lives.

## The Apostles' Ministry

Word of the apostles' awe-inspiring ministry spread throughout Asia Minor. Through the power of the Spirit, Peter and John healed a lame man who had been sitting at the gate of the temple, begging for alms (Acts 3:1–10). Peter then gave an impassioned speech to a crowd gathered in the portico, or "porch," of Solomon, one of only two parts of Solomon's great temple that had not been destroyed (vv. 11–26).

Why was this speaking platform vital to the apostles' mission? Because here, in the shadow of the colonnades, Peter had the opportunity to share the Gospel with lost Jews and Gentiles alike.

---

1. John Eldredge, *Wild at Heart: Discovering the Secret of a Man's Soul* (Nashville, Tenn.: Thomas Nelson Publishers, 2001), p. 200.

2. John Eldredge, *Wild at Heart*, p. 200.

As Peter preached the Gospel, the charred remains of the once-magnificent temple may have reminded the people of their old way of life. But now it was evident that God was doing something new! The Jews and Gentiles who gathered there heard an astonishing message about the promise of new life and freedom in Christ. They finally realized that Jesus of Nazareth truly had been the promised Messiah and that His life, death, and resurrection fulfilled every Old Testament prophecy regarding His ministry. Rejoicing, many in Peter's audience placed their faith in Christ.

But the apostles' obedience to Christ's command had severe consequences! The priests, the Sadducees, and the captain of the temple guard threw Peter and John into jail for "creating a disturbance"—namely, by unashamedly proclaiming the Gospel and healing the sick and lame (Acts 4–5).

Peter and John thrown into jail for preaching the Word? Isn't it amazing to see how the plot of this "book of adventures" unfolds? And, unlike the situations in most action movies, these events *actually occurred*! Wait until you see what happened next:

> But during the night an angel of the Lord opened
> the gates of the prison, and taking them out he said,
> "Go, stand and speak to the people in the temple
> the whole message of this Life." (Acts 5:19–20)

An angel literally opened the gates and set Peter and John free! After their miraculous release from prison, the apostles continued their ministry with renewed vigor. Peter, John, and the others chose seven men to oversee the care of widows and to perform other functions of the church. This way, the apostles would be free to continue speaking the "message of this Life" (v. 20).

## Philip's Ministry in Samaria

Now, let's take a road trip with the apostle Philip to Samaria, where some remarkable events unfolded. Philip proclaimed Christ to the people of Samaria and performed miracles there through the power of the Holy Spirit. Huge crowds lined the dusty roads, calling to Philip and tugging on his robe. They gathered to watch him cast out unclean spirits, restore the sick, and heal the lame in the name of Christ. As a result of his ministry, "there was much rejoicing in that city" (Acts 8:8).

Then a strange thing happened. Philip's ministry caught the

attention of a man named Simon, a sorcerer who had formerly practiced magic in the city. This man had astonished the people of Samaria by "claiming to be great" and performing what seemed to be miraculous deeds (vv. 9–11). Some even said, "This man is what is called the Great Power of God" (v. 10). But Simon's magic was of a different variety, empowered by forces of darkness rather than by the Holy Spirit of God.

Simon knew that his power came from a counterfeit source, Satan. He recognized immediately that this power did not even come close to rivaling the power that Philip had through the Holy Spirit of God! As a result of seeing the extraordinary signs that Philip performed and hearing the Gospel message, Simon confessed faith in Christ and chose to be baptized (v. 13).

Unfortunately, Simon didn't seem to understand exactly how the Holy Spirit worked. He may have accepted the Gospel message solely because he wanted to gain the apostles' ability to perform miracles, signs, and wonders. Greed for miracle-working power began to gnaw at his mind and heart, and he decided to do whatever he could to get this power for himself. He even tried to purchase it (v. 18)!

Peter severely reprimanded Simon, reminding him that the ability to perform miracles was not to be used for personal gain, but to glorify God. This power from the Spirit was certainly not something that could be bought with silver or gold (vv. 18–23)! Simon's heart was humbled after Peter's warning, and he responded, "Pray to the Lord for me yourselves, so that nothing of what you have said may come upon me" (v. 24). We hear nothing more about Simon throughout the rest of Scripture. Hopefully, he learned his lesson and changed his tune!

### Philip's Ministry to the Ethiopian Eunuch

Following this incident, Philip and the other apostles started back on the long trek to Jerusalem, stopping to preach the Gospel in several Samaritan villages along the way:

> So, when they had solemnly testified and spoken the word of the Lord, they started back to Jerusalem, and were preaching the gospel to many villages of the Samaritans. (v. 25)

Then God stepped in to perform another serendipity in Philip's life:

> But an angel of the lord spoke to Philip saying,

"Get up and go south to the road that descends from Jerusalem to Gaza." (This is a desert road.) (v. 26)

You might think that the Lord would have left Philip there in the middle of the action, where the people were eagerly responding to the Lord's message. But God's ways are not our ways! The Lord suddenly called Philip to go in a completely different direction. He had a specific ministry in mind, and Philip was the one to carry it out.

What was Philip's response? When God called him, the apostle exhibited a willing heart and a go-for-it attitude, even though he didn't know exactly what the Lord had in mind. He demonstrated six qualities that are vital for anyone seeking to touch others' lives with the Gospel: *sensitivity, availability, initiative, tactfulness, preciseness, and decisiveness.*

### Sensitivity

> So he got up and went; and there was an Ethiopian eunuch, a court official of Candace, queen of the Ethiopians, who was in charge of all her treasure; and he had come to Jerusalem to worship, and he was returning and sitting in his chariot, and was reading the prophet Isaiah. (vv. 27–28)

Sensitive to the leading of the Holy Spirit, Philip immediately "got up and went" (v. 27). On a lonely stretch of desert road, he met a high-ranking official in the Ethiopian royalty who was reading in his chariot. The eunuch served as the treasurer for the queen mother, Candace, who was the head of the active government of ancient Ethiopia.[3]

The Law prevented eunuchs from actually entering the Lord's assembly to worship (see Deut. 23:1). This man had gone to Jerusalem to worship outside the assembly, in a place where he could overhear the message. While he was there, the eunuch obtained a scroll containing the words of the prophet Isaiah, most likely the Scripture passage the priest had read in the assembly. Evidently, this Ethiopian eunuch was a God-fearer—a worshiper of Yahweh—though he was not a full-fledged convert to Judaism.[4]

---

3. *Candace* was not her literal name, but a title given to the queen mother, as the title *Pharaoh* was used to refer to the king of Egypt. John F. Walvoord and Roy B. Zuck, eds., *The Bible Knowledge Commentary*, New Testament ed. (Wheaton, Ill.: Victor Books, 1989), p. 374.

4. John F. Walvoord and Roy B. Zuck, eds., *The Bible Knowledge Commentary*, p. 374.

Philip was sensitive to the Spirit's leading and discerned the eunuch's desire to understand Scripture. Like Philip, when we're in tune with the Holy Spirit, we have a greater passion to obey God, and we're more open to divine appointments.

### Availability

This eunuch was no doubt a wise man, well educated in the ways of the world. But he needed Philip's help to be able to understand the things of God. Here, the obedient apostle demonstrated another principle necessary for touching others' lives: *availability*.

> Then the Spirit said to Philip, "Go up and join this chariot." Philip ran up and heard him reading Isaiah the prophet, and said, "Do you understand what you are reading?" And he said, "Well, how could I, unless someone guides me?" And he invited Philip to come up and sit with him. (vv. 29–31)

Now Philip understood why the Holy Spirit had suddenly diverted him onto a path in the middle of the desert! Had he been unavailable—preoccupied with his own agenda, activities, or worries—he would have missed out on a life-changing opportunity. Philip's adventure had suddenly gained purpose and perspective.

At the eunuch's invitation, Philip eagerly clambered up into the chariot.

> Now the passage of Scripture which he was reading was this:
> "He was led as a sheep to slaughter;
> And as a lamb before its shearer is silent,
> So He does not open His mouth.
> In humiliation His judgment was taken away;
> Who will relate His generation?
> For His life is removed from the earth."
> The eunuch answered Philip and said, "Please tell me, of whom does the prophet say this? Of himself or of someone else?" Then Philip opened his mouth, and beginning from this Scripture he preached Jesus to him. (vv. 32–35)

The eunuch understood that this prophecy referred to a particular person's ministry, but he wasn't sure whose. He was probably familiar with the prophecies regarding the Messiah, but evidently he didn't realize that the Messiah had already come!

This passage from Isaiah 53:7–8 holds extraordinary historical significance. Often referred to as one of the four "Servant Songs" in the book, it portrays the suffering of the prophet Isaiah and a righteous remnant of Jewish believers. It also prophesies the future Messiah as the suffering Servant who bore the weight of the sins of the world on his shoulders. Philip shared the Gospel story from the perspective of one who had been right there in the middle of the action, watching these extraordinary events occur in the life of Christ as the prophecies of Isaiah came to fruition.

### Initiative

Philip took the opportunity to touch the eunuch's life in another way. He ran up to him and asked the question "Do you understand what you are reading?" Philip didn't offend the eunuch or put him down for not knowing; he asked a neutral question and walked through the open door that God provided. He showed *initiative*.

The eunuch's heart leaped as he heard the Gospel message clearly for the first time and understood that Jesus, the Messiah, had come. The long lists of Jewish regulations that had kept him on the fringe of religious circles finally gave way as he established a relationship with the living God.

> As they went along the road they came to some water; and the eunuch said, "Look! Water! What prevents me from being baptized?" And Philip said, "If you believe with all your heart, you may." And he answered and said, "I believe that Jesus Christ is the Son of God." And he ordered the chariot to stop; and they both went down into the water, Philip as well as the eunuch, and he baptized him. (vv. 36–38)

When we take the initiative to act on God's directives, He uses us to perform serendipities in the lives of others.

### Tactfulness

Did you notice what Philip did first? He tactfully and sensitively determined the man's need. He saw that the Ethiopian eunuch was reading from the book of Isaiah, asked him a question, and then waited for an answer and an invitation before joining him in his chariot.

What do you think would have happened if Philip had immediately jumped into this man's chariot and started preaching? The encounter might have ended in disaster!

Although Philip clearly had a divine appointment with the eunuch, he didn't push his way into the situation. He demonstrated *tactfulness*.

### Preciseness

As a result of Philip's *precise* teaching through the Spirit, the light of Christ illuminated the eunuch's mind and heart. For the first time, this man understood that the passage he had been reading described Christ and the sufferings He had endured to save humanity from sin.

### Decisiveness

The Ethiopian official had heard the Gospel message and was prepared to make a decision for Christ. He saw some water and earnestly desired to be baptized (v. 36). But Philip was quick to verbally confirm what was happening in the man's heart. He said, "If you believe with all your heart, you may [be baptized]." And the eunuch replied with, "I believe that Jesus Christ is the Son of God" (v. 37). Philip prompted the eunuch to make a *decisive* commitment to Christ—one that left no room for error, confusion, or wavering. It was essential that the eunuch understand that it was not baptism that would save him, but faith.

## Philip Is Snatched Away

The eunuch was baptized immediately. God performed a miracle in his heart that day, but He wasn't finished yet. Look what happened next!

> When they came up out of the water, the Spirit of the Lord snatched Philip away; and the eunuch no longer saw him, but went on his way rejoicing. (v. 39)

Unbelievable! As soon as the eunuch emerged from his baptism, Philip disappeared. At first, the Ethiopian official must have been stunned at this astonishing turn of events. He must have looked around, rubbed his eyes, and thought, *Was this a dream?* Philip had appeared out of nowhere, explained the mysteries of God, and then vanished without a trace! But the eunuch recognized that he had been chosen for a rare encounter with a messenger of the living God, and he "went on his way rejoicing" (v. 39).

The eunuch wasn't the only one who was surprised! The Spirit of the Lord "snatched Philip away" and placed him at Azotus, which was several days' journey southeast of Samaria, where he had been talking with the eunuch just moments before. There, encouraged by his miraculous encounter with the eunuch, Philip kept preaching:

> But Philip found himself at Azotus, and as he passed through he kept preaching the gospel to all the cities until he came to Caesarea. (v. 40)

When Philip first decided to follow Christ, he never knew that his journey would include time travel! And this was only one of the incredible adventures that he experienced along the way. Sometimes we forget that Philip and the other apostles *really knew* Jesus. They lived side by side, day in and day out, with the Son of God. Their sandals kicked up clouds of reddish dust as they walked long miles together. They grilled fish and ate bread together around campfires on chilly evenings as waves lapped against the shore. They celebrated happy occasions and wept bitterly at others. They truly *shared* their lives with each other.

After Jesus ascended to heaven, the apostles banded together and committed themselves to taking His message of love throughout the world. As they witnessed miracle after miracle, they grew to understand the reality of God's love even more deeply. These adventurous and faithful men faced adventures and dangers we would never even dream of, all for one purpose—to touch others' lives with the Gospel.

 *Living Insights*

In his book *Wild at Heart*, John Eldredge writes:

> If you had permission to do what you really want to do, what would you do? Don't ask *how*; that will cut your desire off at the knees. *How* is never the right question; *how* is a faithless question. It means "unless I can see my way clearly I won't believe it, won't venture forth." . . . *How* is God's department. He is asking you *what*. What is written in your

heart? What makes you come alive? If you could do what you've always wanted to do, what would it be?"[5]

As you reflect on this passage from Eldredge's book, answer the following questions:

What would you do if you could do *anything*? (Remember, don't ask *how*, just *what*.) List several personal goals or dreams that you have.

_____

_____

_____

_____

_____

_____

What has kept you from pursuing these dreams in the past?

_____

_____

_____

_____

What frustrations have you felt in your own life as you have tried to achieve these goals? What methods has Satan used to thwart your efforts or derail your focus?

_____

_____

_____

_____

5. John Eldredge, *Wild at Heart*, p. 206.

What have you learned from the examples of the apostles about adventure and pursuing God's call for your life? How can you apply these principles to your pursuit of your particular dreams and goals?

_____

_____

_____

_____

_____

_____

List three things you can do *today* to start pursuing your dreams and goals. Find an accountability partner who will pray with and for you. Keep track of your accomplishments together.

1. _____

_____

2. _____

_____

3. _____

_____

## Chapter 4

# BEING TRANSFORMED

### Acts 9:1–22

Alan Redpath once said, "The conversion of a soul is the miracle of a moment, but the manufacture of a saint is the task of a lifetime."[1]

Isn't it interesting that the more notorious an individual, the more skeptical we are about embracing his or her conversion as "the miracle of a moment"? Often we keep on the fringe of our Christian circles those who have lived wayward lives until they really *prove* that they've gained new life in Christ. Why? Because we sometimes doubt that the Lord has completely transformed a person's life. Instead of thinking, "Wow! What a miracle!" we tend to think, "Hmmm . . . I'm not too sure." Instead of extending grace, we often wait to see some good works so we can be "extra sure" that the person is truly saved.

When we're skeptical about someone's spiritual conversion, we minimize the miracle that God has done in his or her life. The next time you're tempted to doubt, remind yourself of this: God is in the life-transforming business. In fact, that's the message of the Gospel!

Chuck Colson served as one of President Richard Nixon's henchmen during the controversial Watergate scandal. During the fallout from Watergate in 1973, a friend shared the Gospel with Colson. As a result, he confessed his sin and placed his faith in Jesus Christ. His conversion was certainly "the miracle of a moment"! Back in 1973, many doubted its sincerity. The *Boston Globe* reported, "If Mr. Colson can repent of his sins, there just has to be hope for everybody."[2] In 1974, Colson pleaded guilty to obstruction of justice and served a seven-month prison term for his involvement with Watergate.

Despite the initial doubts of the public, Chuck Colson demonstrated that God's call on his life was real. After his release from prison, he and three friends launched Prison Fellowship Ministries to help meet the spiritual and physical needs of prisoners and their

---

1. Alan Redpath, *The Making of a Man of God: Studies in the Life of David* (Westwood, N.J.: Fleming H. Revell Co., n.d.).

2. "About Charles W. Colson," accessed on October 7, 2002, available at www.pfm.org.

families. Over the past twenty-five years, Prison Fellowship Ministries has grown into the world's largest prison outreach, ministering in eighty-eight countries worldwide, including the United States. Colson still serves as head of the organization, and he is also a prolific writer and popular speaker.[3] Clearly, the Lord is still in the business of "manufacturing saints" out of sinners! After all, isn't that what He is doing with each of us?

Like Chuck Colson, Saul of Tarsus was also a celebrity of sorts, notorious as one of the most outspoken and violent God-haters that ever walked the earth. He was consumed with his task of destroying Christians:

> Now Saul, still breathing threats and murder against the disciples of the Lord, went to the high priest, and asked for letters from him to the synagogues at Damascus, so that if he found any belonging to the Way, both men and women, he might bring them bound to Jerusalem. (Acts 9:1–2)

Like a furious fire-breathing dragon awakened from a centuries-long sleep, Saul "breathed threats and murder" against Christ's followers. As a Roman citizen, a full-blooded Jew, and a Pharisee, Saul self-righteously "ravaged the church" (Acts 8:3), tackling each persecution project with passion and determination. He ordered men as well as women to be flogged and thrown into prison. He also cast his vote against many believers who were then tortured and put to death.

The gospel writer Luke recorded these words of Saul in Acts 22:4–5:

> I persecuted this Way to the death, binding and putting both men and women into prisons, as also the high priest and all the Council of the elders can testify. From them I also received letters to the brethren, and started off for Damascus in order to bring even those who were there to Jerusalem as prisoners to be punished.

Saul's cruelty as a persecutor of Christians was widely known. Aggressive, powerful, and fearless, he actually *delighted* in putting

---

3. "About Charles W. Colson," at www.pfm.org.

to death these followers of "the Way." Yet God, in His infinite love, was pursuing Saul even more fervently than Saul was chasing down believers. This Pharisee would not be able to elude God's grasp forever. Saul didn't know it yet, but he was destined for glory!

## Seven Steps of Saul's Conversion

As Saul rushed from Jerusalem to Damascus to deliver his letters of condemnation, the Lord suddenly stopped him in his tracks. Saul had a close encounter of the supernatural kind with the risen Christ! As God intervened in Saul's life, seven events occurred, including some fantastic divine phenomena.

### A Light Shone

> As he was traveling, it happened that he was approaching Damascus, and suddenly a light from heaven flashed around him. (9:3)

A blinding light from heaven stopped Saul in his tracks. Piercing and laser-like in its intensity, this light was even more powerful than the desert sun at midday. Though this passage doesn't explicitly say that Saul "saw Christ," this fact is implied in his reference in verse 3 to the blinding *shekinah* glory, the light from heaven indicative of the Lord's presence. Several other passages declare that he actually saw the Lord (see Acts 9:17, 27; 26:16; 1 Cor. 9:1; 15:8).

One of the qualifications of an apostle was that he had to have seen the risen Jesus after His resurrection. On the Damascus road, Saul met the resurrected Lord in all His glory, receiving the call and the stamp of approval to become an apostle.

### Saul Fell to the Ground

Terrified at the sight of this blinding heavenly phenomenon, Saul

> . . . fell to the ground . . . (9:4a)

He had no idea what was happening to him or who this mysterious Stranger might have been.

### A Voice Spoke

Then Saul heard a voice from heaven

> . . . saying to him, "Saul, Saul, why are you persecuting Me?" (9:4b)

Note that Jesus said, "Why are you persecuting *Me?*" and not "Why are you persecuting my followers?" Saul's terror tactics not only destroyed Christians; they were an affront to Jesus Himself. The Lord let Saul know that his brutal attacks on the church were also attacks on Him, the risen Savior.

### Saul Responded

Stunned, Saul reeled in shock as he heard Jesus' question. Still blinded by the light and confused by the voice from heaven, he fearfully inquired regarding the identity of this mysterious Stranger:

And he said, "Who are you, Lord?" (9:5a)

### Jesus Identified Himself

Then Saul received the Lord's answer:

And He said, "I am Jesus whom you are persecuting."
(9:5b)

Can you imagine Saul's amazement when he heard this state-ment from the mouth of the Lord? His heart must have filled with unspeakable terror as he began to understand that he had been persecuting Someone that he shouldn't have been!

### Saul Responded Again

Fearfully and humbly, Saul asked another question:

And I said, "What shall I do, Lord?" (Acts 22:10)

Saul had been so blinded by his hatred that only the piercing light of the *shekinah* glory could make him see through spiritual eyes. His ears had been closed to the message of the Gospel for so long that only the Lord's voice could enable him to hear the Word. Jesus definitely had Saul's full attention, and Saul knew that he had to offer up his life to the Lord.

### Jesus Answered

Jesus answered Saul's question by telling him where to go next:

"Get up and enter the city, and it will be told you what you must do." (9:6)

Saul waited to hear more, but that was it! The voice stopped as quickly as it had begun, and the light vanished as suddenly as it had appeared. Saul and his men were left alone with nothing else to do but follow the Lord's command.

> The men who traveled with him stood speechless, hearing the voice but seeing no one. Saul got up from the ground, and though his eyes were open, he could see nothing; and leading him by the hand, they brought him into Damascus. And he was three days without sight, and neither ate nor drank. (9:7–9)

What a traumatic, yet miraculous experience! In his ode "The Hound of Heaven," poet Francis Thompson depicted God as a divine "Hound," fervently pursuing a relationship with His beloved children.[4] Now Saul knew firsthand how it felt to be the cunning "fox" chased by the "Hound of Heaven"! Hot on Saul's trail, Jesus pursued this man who was foolishly trying to outrun Him. Finally, He appeared to Saul on the Damascus road. The running stopped. The chase ended. The divine Hound caught the fox.

## Saul Becomes Paul

In biblical times, names held great importance. Parents selected their children's names carefully, reflecting their own hopes regarding the spirituality, personality, appearance, character, and desired attributes of their offspring.

Sometimes people changed their names as a result of a particular spiritual experience or turning point in their lives. Saul changed his name after his conversion to reflect the remarkable transformation that he had undergone. Luke recorded this in Acts 13:9:

> "But Saul, who was also known as Paul . . ."

The name *Saul* came from the Hebrew term *shā'ûl*, which means "asked for."[5] Remember King Saul from the Old Testament, who was "asked for" by the people? The Israelites demanded a king in order to suit their own desires, so God gave them one. But He warned them ahead of time that King Saul's reign would have tragic results.

---

4. Francis Thompson, "The Hound of Heaven," accessed on October 8, 2002, available at at http://www.houndsofheaven.com/thepoem.htm.

5. Merrill F. Unger, *The New Unger's Bible Dictionary*, rev. ed., ed. R.K. Harrison (Chicago, Ill.: Moody Press, 1988), see "Saul."

In contrast with the connotations of the name *Saul*, the name *Paul* means "little" in Greek.[6] Certain writers suggest that Saul was short of stature, so this Greek nickname may have referred partly to his height. But the name change also reflected the shift in Paul's priorities:

> It is best to understand that Saul's name was changed as a matter of course *when he became a Christian*, that the word *Paul* means "little," and that Paul wanted to be known as the "Little One" in Christ's service; such changes in the cases of Abram, Gideon, Naomi, etc., are to be noted.[7]

Several biblical figures took new names to reflect certain aspects of their personal and spiritual journeys. Some were even renamed by God Himself! Though his new name meant "little," Saul-turned-Paul embraced the Gospel message with a huge passion. As a result of this apostle's ministry in the following years, the kingdom of God reaped a harvest of souls too numerous to count.

## Four Events Following Saul's Conversion

After Saul's miraculous encounter with the risen Christ on the Damascus road, four events occurred. He *saw a vision, made a contact, formed a relationship*, and *made a proclamation*.

### He Saw A Vision

God called a disciple named Ananias to fulfill the vision He had given Saul:

> Now there was a disciple at Damascus named Ananias; and the Lord said to him in a vision, "Ananias." And he said, "Here I am, Lord." And the Lord said to him, "Get up and go to the street called Straight, and inquire at the house of Judas for a man from Tarsus named Saul, for he is praying, and he has seen in a vision a man named Ananias come in and lay his hands on him, so that he might regain his sight." (Acts 9:10–12)

6. Unger, *The New Unger's Bible Dictionary*, see "Paul."
7. Unger, *The New Unger's Bible Dictionary*, see "Paul."

Can you imagine? God asked his faithful disciple Ananias to meet Saul, a bloodthirsty mass-murderer of Christians, and lay his hands on him so that he could see again! Naturally, the terrified Ananias feared for his life:

> But Ananias answered, "Lord, I have heard from many about this man, how much harm he did to Your saints at Jerusalem; and here he has authority from the chief priests to bind all who call on Your name." (vv. 13–14)

Ananias thought, *I must be hearing things!* At first, he doubted the Lord's plan. But the divine Hound had chosen a zealous fox named Saul to be an instrument of His righteousness, and Ananias was just the one to bear the news:

> But the Lord said to him, "Go, for he is a chosen instrument of Mine, to bear My name before the Gentiles and kings and the sons of Israel; for I will show him how much he must suffer for My name's sake." (vv. 15–16)

### He Made a Contact

Obediently, Ananias left to meet Saul, despite his own fears:

> So Ananias departed and entered the house, and after laying hands on him said, "Brother Saul, the Lord Jesus, who appeared to you on the road by which you were coming, has sent me so that you may regain your sight and be filled with the Holy Spirit." And immediately there fell from his eyes something like scales, and he regained his sight, and he got up and was baptized; and he took food and was strengthened. (vv. 17–19)

Finally, the scales fell from Saul's eyes, and he could see again. The blindness had been a very real reminder of the Lord's divine intervention. Unable to see, Saul was dependent upon others—something that he definitely wasn't used to! This period of blindness and fasting forced him to think deeply about what had happened on the Damascus road. Humbled, he chose to be baptized as soon as he could see again. He also ate in order to regain his strength for the monumental events that he knew lay ahead.

### He Formed a Relationship

> Now for several days he was with the disciples who
> were at Damascus . . . (v. 19b)

Saul spent several days recovering from his incredible encounter
and learning from the Christians in Damascus.

### He Gave a Proclamation

> . . . and immediately he began to proclaim Jesus in
> the synagogues, saying, "He is the Son of God." (v. 20)

Saul couldn't wait to proclaim the Good News, and he immediately started to share the life-altering message of the Gospel with
others. You can imagine the crowd's amazement as they heard this
violent Christian-hater proclaiming that Jesus was the Messiah! At
first, Christians distrusted him, thinking maybe his conversion was
a trick. And the religious Jews weren't too sure either!

> All those hearing him continued to be amazed, and
> were saying, "Is this not he who in Jerusalem de-
> stroyed those who called on this name, and who had
> come here for the purpose of bringing them bound
> before the chief priests?" But Saul kept increasing
> in strength and confounding the Jews who lived at
> Damascus by proving that this Jesus is the Christ.
> (vv. 21–22)

Those around Saul may have doubted at first that he had genu-
inely experienced a radical life change, but eventually they had to
concede that he was the real deal! He now preached the Gospel
with the same zeal he had once used to hunt down Christians.

Saul's conversion, like that of so many others, represented "the
miracle of a moment." The Lord instantly transformed a hateful,
sin-sick Pharisee into a lover of God. Saul was a new creation in
Jesus Christ. The chase had ended, and God had won!

 *Living Insights*

In Acts 26:14, Saul-turned-Paul recorded another unusual
aspect of his conversation with the Lord on the Damascus road.

> "And when we had all fallen to the ground, I heard

a voice saying to me in the Hebrew dialect, 'Saul, Saul, why are you persecuting me? It is hard for you to kick against the goads.'"

"Kick against the goads"? What did this mean? One commentator notes,

> Saul's rage was the more deeply inflamed by the thrusts of an uneasy conscience, which is the only explanation of his 'kicking against the goads' (26:14). Conversions such as this are not produced in a psychological vacuum.[8]

In other words, Saul's conscience had been pricking him as he persecuted Christians. The horrible suffering of these faithful believers haunted him when he lay down to sleep at night. Their forgiveness and kind words in the face of flogging and merciless torture pierced his soul with guilt. Their willingness to die for their faith made him wonder if maybe, just maybe, the message of the Gospel was true.

Have you ever felt the "goads" of the Holy Spirit? If so, what happened, and what was your response?

_____

_____

_____

_____

Has the Lord completely transformed your life like He did Saul's? If so, write out your own "miracle of a moment" conversion story here.

_____

_____

_____

8. F. F. Bruce, ed., *The International Bible Commentary*, rev. ed. (Grand Rapids, Mich.: Marshall Morgan and Scott Publications Ltd., Zondervan Publishing House, 1986), p. 1284.

_____

_____

_____

_____

_____

_____

_____

_____

_____

    If you don't have a "miracle story" and feel unsure about your relationship with God, you may be feeling the same "goading" from the Holy Spirit that Saul felt. If this is true of you, don't delay! God wants to transform your life through the love of His Son, Jesus Christ. Seek out a person or a place where you can go to receive more information about becoming a true Christ-follower. You may speak to one of our pastors on staff by calling the Insight for Living Care Line at (972) 473-5097, or you may write us at Insight for Living, Pastoral Ministries Department, P.O. Box 269000, Plano, TX 75026-9000.

## Chapter 5

# PREVAILING THROUGH PRAYER

### Acts 12:1–17

A boy named Cole sent this letter home from Boy Scout camp:

> Dear Mom,
>
> Our scoutmaster told us all to write to our parents in case you saw the flood on TV and worried. We are OK. Only 1 of our tents and 2 sleeping bags got washed away. Luckily, none of us got drowned because we were all up on the mountain looking for Chad when it happened. Oh yes, please call Chad's mother and tell her he is OK. He can't write because of the cast. . . .
>
> Scoutmaster Webb got mad at Chad for going on a hike alone without telling anyone. Chad said he did tell him, but it was during the fire so he probably didn't hear him. Did you know that if you put gas on a fire, the gas can will blow up? The wet wood still didn't burn, but one of our tents did. Also some of our clothes. . . .
>
> We will be home on Saturday if Scoutmaster Webb gets the car fixed. It wasn't his fault about the wreck. . . .
>
> Scoutmaster Webb is a neat guy. Don't worry, he is a good driver. In fact, he is teaching Terry how to drive. But he only lets him drive on the mountain roads where there isn't any traffic. . . .
>
> Also Wade and I threw up. Scoutmaster Webb said it probably was just food poisoning from the leftover chicken, he said they got sick that way with the food they ate in prison. I'm so glad he got out and became our scoutmaster. . . .
>
> I have to go now. We are going into town to

mail our letters and buy bullets. Don't worry about
anything. We are fine.

Love, Cole[1]

Can you imagine getting a letter like this from your child? Cole's
mother must have wondered whether to laugh or cry! She probably
got down on her knees and prayed like never before. We've all had
similar experiences, haven't we? Sometimes our circumstances just
don't turn out the way we expect. But God uses every situation,
good or bad, to draw us closer to Him. Difficulties, setbacks, and
surprises cause us to ask, "Lord, what should I do now? What do I
need to learn from this situation? What's the next step?" Our serendipities are just part of the fun of adventuring with God!

God specializes in the impossible. There's *nothing* He can't do!
Yet we're often slow to trust Him. Only a proper *perspective* can
offer us inner peace in the midst of life's impossibilities. And only
through consistent, fervent prayer can we gain this godly perspective on our lives.

God unleashes His power through our prayers, working miracles
and performing serendipities that we never dreamed of. The Lord
proves Himself faithful when we seek Him—even in the toughest
circumstances and the most impossible situations. God's miracle-
working power might seem distant or theoretical at times, but it's
not. It's *real*!

The Acts of the Apostles proves it, teeming with true stories
of supernatural encounters and glorious serendipities. Let's turn to
Acts 12 to discover how God used intercessory prayer to perform
an incredible miracle in the life of Peter, the fisherman-turned-
apostle.

## An Initial Orientation

The events took place during a time of great turmoil and persecution of Christians:

> Now about that time Herod the king laid hands
> on some who belonged to the church in order to
> mistreat them. And he had James the brother of
> John put to death with a sword. (Acts 12:1–2)

---

1. "Boy Scout Letter from Camp," accessed on October 14, 2002, available at http://www.gcfl.net.

Believers felt fearful and discouraged as Herod Agrippa persecuted Christians, ordering that they be tortured and put to death. Herod even had the apostle James killed to please the Jewish leaders. One writer notes,

> [Herod] was exceedingly ambitious to please his Jewish subjects, and this passion led him to become a persecutor of the Christians in the little community at Jerusalem.[2]

When Herod perceived the Jews' joy at having James out of the way, he made another move against the Christian community:

> When he saw that it pleased the Jews, he proceeded to arrest Peter also. Now it was during the days of Unleavened Bread. (Acts 12:3)

Like starving hawks swooping down to snatch their prey, Herod's guards quickly arrested Peter and threw him in prison. No trials, sentencing, or executions of any kind could be carried out during the time of the Feast of Unleavened Bread, so Herod planned to wait out the feast week and then have Peter executed as soon as the festival ended. His plot involved wiping out all the leaders of the Christian faith by arresting and killing them one by one. But God had other plans!

## An Impossible Situation

> When he had seized [Peter] he put him in prison, delivering him to four squads of soldiers to guard him, intending after the Passover to bring him out before the people. (v. 4)

Four squads of soldiers? That's a lot of guards! Herod was well aware of the miracles and healings that God was doing through the disciples. The conniving king tried to hedge his bets by tightening security, but deep down he feared that even his fierce Roman guards were no match for the living God. One author notes:

> Herod's insecurity in taking this step became obvious when he ordered Peter to be guarded "by

2. Merrill F. Unger, *The New Unger's Bible Dictionary*, rev. ed., ed. R.K. Harrison (Chicago, Ill.: Moody Press, 1988), p. 563, see "Herod."

four squads of four soldiers each" (12:4). Why 16 men to guard a fisherman turned preacher? Herod knew he was not dealing with an ordinary movement or ordinary people. There was every evidence that something supernatural was taking place. This was not the first time one of the apostles had been arrested and put in jail. On one occasion the apostles had been miraculously released from jail by an angel of the Lord. The next day their accusers discovered them teaching God's Word in the temple (5:17–21). This time Herod was taking no chances.[3]

As soon as they heard that Herod's guards had arrested Peter, the believers in Jerusalem gathered together to pray earnestly for him:

So Peter was kept in the prison, but prayer for him was being made fervently by the church to God. (Acts 12:5)

One of the greatest adventures we can undertake is concerted, deliberate, specific intercessory prayer for others who are in need. God uses our prayers in mighty ways that surprise even the most faithful among us! And these Christians were no exception. Peter's brothers and sisters in Christ fell to their knees, praying through the night for Peter's protection and deliverance. They passionately interceded for this faithful apostle, yet we will later see that they had little faith that God would spare Peter's life. They fully expected Peter to meet the same dire end as the apostle James.

On the very night when Herod was about to bring him forward, Peter was sleeping between two soldiers, bound with two chains, and guards in front of the door were watching over the prison. (v. 6)

Normally, a prison guard chained his prisoner's right hand to his own left hand to prevent the possibility of escape. But Herod took no chances with Peter! The king attempted to "double his luck" by having the apostle bound with two heavy chains and guarded by two Roman soldiers while the other guards kept a vigilant watch over Peter's cell door. Escape was absolutely impossible . . . or was it?

3. Gene A. Getz, *Praying for One Another* (Wheaton, Ill.: Victor Books, a division of SP Publications, 1983), p. 81.

## A Miraculous Intervention

> And behold, an angel of the Lord suddenly appeared
> and a light shone in the cell; and he struck Peter's
> side and woke him up, saying, "Get up quickly." And
> his chains fell off his hands. And the angel said to
> him, "Gird yourself and put on your sandals." And
> he did so. And he said to him, "Wrap your cloak
> around you and follow me." (vv. 7–8)

God heard the intercessory prayers of His people, and He answered with an extraordinary miracle. A glorious messenger of the
Lord suddenly appeared, illuminating Peter's cell with brilliant light.
The thick iron chains around Peter's wrists snapped like threads
and fell to the floor. At the angel's urging, Peter quickly arose,
dressed, and followed him out of the crowded, heavily guarded
Roman prison.

Clearly, God had purposes for Peter that had not yet been fully
accomplished. He wanted Peter to continue proclaiming the Gospel
in the streets and shouting the truth from the portico of Solomon.
The hopeless, the brokenhearted, the lame, the blind, the deaf, and
the mute still needed to hear Peter's message and experience God's
healing touch. Peter had a job to do, and there was no time to waste!

> And [Peter] went out and continued to follow, and he
> did not know that what was being done by the angel
> was real, but thought he was seeing a vision. (v. 9)

An angel of the Lord? Iron chains falling to the ground? A light
brighter than the desert sun appearing in a dank, cold prison cell?
No guards, no alerts, and no shouts? This fabulous miracle had Peter
convinced that he must be dreaming. He thought that God must
be granting Him a vision of a most unusual sort.

> When they had passed the first and second guard,
> they came to the iron gate that leads into the city,
> which opened for them by itself; and they went out
> and went along one street, and immediately the an-
> gel departed from him. (v. 10)

The angel left as quickly as he had come, leaving Peter standing
alone on the dark, narrow streets of Jerusalem. Reality set in as
Peter felt the chill of the night breeze against his face. As his eyes
adjusted from the brightness of the angel's presence to the pitch-

black night, he acknowledged that a true miracle had occurred. God had delivered him from prison.

> When Peter came to himself, he said, "Now I know for sure that the Lord has sent forth His angel and rescued me from the hand of Herod and from all that the Jewish people were expecting." (v. 11)

## Their Natural Reaction

As soon as Peter came to his senses, he rushed to greet the Jerusalem believers. He wanted to celebrate with those who had prayed so fervently for his deliverance!

> And when he realized this, he went to the house of Mary, the mother of John who was also called Mark, where many were gathered together and were praying. When he knocked at the door of the gate, a servant-girl named Rhoda came to answer. When she recognized Peter's voice, because of her joy she did not open the gate, but ran in and announced that Peter was standing in front of the gate. They said to her, "You are out of your mind!" But she kept insisting that it was so. (vv. 12–15b)

These believers had willingly come before God's throne in prayer for their brother Peter. They had prayed for a miracle. Why, then, were they so surprised when God granted their request? Let's examine the three responses of these individuals to learn what *not* to say when God answers our prayers.

### Three Responses

The believers' first response was, "You are out of your mind!" (v. 15a). They had prayed for Peter's deliverance, but they never really expected it to happen! They thought that Rhoda, the little servant girl, must be seeing things.

The believers' second response was, "It is his angel" (v. 15). They thought that if an apparition resembling Peter was actually at the door, it must be his "angel," or his ghost—meaning his spirit. They assumed that he had already been killed by Herod's executioners.

The believers' third response was amazement:

> But Peter continued knocking; and when they had

opened the door, they saw him and were amazed. But motioning to them with his hand to be silent, he described to them how the Lord had led him out of the prison. And he said, "Report these things to James and the brethren." Then he left and went to another place. (vv. 16–17)

Finally, they got it. Peter was alive, the recipient of a serendipitous experience like no other! Through this miraculous series of events, God taught Peter, the other apostles, and the believers in the Jerusalem community an important lesson about prayer and faith. When we intercede for someone else, we're called to do so with the faith that God will answer. He doesn't always answer our prayers in the way we wish, but His perfect will is done in all things. Someone has said, "We are continually faced with a series of great opportunities brilliantly disguised as insoluble problems."[4] But God is Master of the impossible. Never underestimate the power of prayer!

 ## Living Insights

Angels perform some of God's most miraculous serendipities and incredible rescues. As messengers sent directly from Him, angels play an important part in our faith. Yet today's culture often makes unbiblical, mystical claims regarding the ministry of angels.

God created Lucifer and the other angels to worship and serve Him. But Lucifer chafed at being second in command. He felt unsatisfied with being subordinate to his Creator, and his pride and covetousness grew. Finally, Lucifer rebelled openly against God in an attempt to usurp the Father's throne for himself. As a result, God cast Lucifer down from heaven, along with one-third of the angels—all those who had turned their backs on God by participating in Lucifer's rebellion. The other two-thirds of the angels remain as holy messengers of God, carrying out the Lord's work and protecting believers against Satan and his demons.

To gain a biblical perspective on the attributes and ministry of angels, let's examine what Scripture says about them.

---

4. John. W. Gardner, accessed October 25, 2002, available at www.quotationspage.com/quotes.php3?author+john+w.+gardner.

First of all, angels are *real*, created by God. Angels possess supernatural knowledge, powers, and abilities that enable them to carry out the Lord's work. However, they are not omniscient as God is (see 2 Sam. 14:20; Mark 13:32).

Angels are invisible unless they are performing a particular task for which they must be seen. As ministering spirits, angels differ from humans, yet they may manifest themselves in human form. Angels do not participate in certain human activities such as marriage and sexual union (see Matt. 22:30). Angels are created by God, not born as humans are. Angels also do not seem to age or die, according to Scripture. However, in some instances recorded in the Bible, angels did eat (see Psalm 78:25; Gen. 18:8; 19:3).

Christians are instructed *not* to worship angels or pray to them. Angels are not deity. We should not confuse them with God the Father, Jesus the Son, or the Holy Spirit (see Heb. 1:3–5; 13–14). Additionally, angels do not experience salvation in the same way that we do when we establish a relationship with Jesus Christ. God's holy, ministering angels do not sin. Therefore, unlike man, they have no need of redemption. In contrast, the fallen angels (demons) that chose to follow Satan will not ever be redeemed, according to Scripture.

Angels are not omnipresent; they can only be in one place at a time. Therefore, not all of them worship around God's throne at every moment. They spend part of their time carrying out God's plan and purposes throughout the world.[5]

What have you learned about the ministry of angels by studying their encounters with Saul, Peter, and other biblical figures?

_____

_____

_____

_____

How is the ministry of angels important in the lives of believers today?

_____

5. Portions of this section were adapted from: Billy Graham, *Angels: God's Secret Agents* (New York, N.Y.: Doubleday Books, 1975), pp. 40–61.

_____

_____

How does the biblical view of angels differ from the world's view?

_____

_____

_____

_____

_____

Have you ever felt the presence or protection of angels in your own life? If so, how?

_____

_____

_____

_____

_____

## Chapter 6

# ADJUSTING TO CHANGE
### Acts 13:1–4

Obedience to God requires openness to change.

Webster's defines the verb *change* as "to make different in some particular."[1] Change is one of life's rare certainties! Our habits change. Our living situations change. Our careers change. Our families change. Our goals change. Our lifestyles change. And when any of these circumstances change, we change! We aren't exactly the same people we were last week, and we won't be exactly the same next week, either. With each day and each experience, we grow to become different people.

## Stepping Out in Faith

As our lives overflow with serendipities and surprises, we welcome some changes and agonize over others. The early Christian leaders—apostles, prophets, and teachers—also struggled to adjust to change. In Acts 13:1–4, we read the account of a difficult turn of events in the lives of several men who had banded together in ministry. Let's first take a look at the nature of their relationship.

> Now there were at Antioch, in the church that was there, prophets and teachers: Barnabas, and Simeon who was called Niger, and Lucius of Cyrene, and Manaen who had been brought up with Herod the tetrarch, and Saul. (Acts 13:1)

These five men worked as a "band of brothers" in the faith, bound by their commitment to God and their zeal to share the Gospel message. As church leaders, they had the responsibility of guarding, instructing, and shepherding their flocks. They were also fast friends, reclining at dinner together, savoring grilled fish, bread, and fragrant wine. They enjoyed close fellowship and sweet communion together and celebrated the victories of their ministry.

---

1. *Merriam-Webster's Collegiate Dictionary*, 10th ed. (Springfield, Mass.: Merriam-Webster, Inc., 2000), see "change."

But that wasn't all. These men also toiled in the trenches, enduring unfathomable pain and difficulty. They were defamed, belittled, and persecuted. They wept bitterly over the griefs, failures, and losses experienced by their small faith community. Some of these men even endured beatings, whippings, and torture. But their *koinonia*, their common experience of faith in God, involved sharing the physical and emotional hardships of their ministry as well as the joys.

## Facing Change

As the apostles ministered together, God chose to abruptly send two of them, Barnabas and Saul, in a different direction:

> While they were ministering to the Lord and fasting, the Holy Spirit said, "Set apart for Me Barnabas and Saul for the work to which I have called them." Then, when they had fasted and prayed and laid their hands on them, they sent them away. (vv. 2–3)

We've all despaired over changes in our relationships. Perhaps your once-loving marriage ended in a bitter divorce. You may have lost a beloved spouse or child. Perhaps you've lost your job or you've had to leave a place where you felt at home. Maybe you've lost a vibrant church family due to a move or a church split. Perhaps you miss spending time with a particular best friend or group of friends. If so, you know the feelings of pain, loss, and discouragement that come when something great ends.

The good news is that even in these hard times, God loves us, and He has a specific plan for each of our lives. When your relationships are struggling, remember this powerful promise:

> And we know that God causes all things to work together for good to those who love God, to those who are called according to His purpose. (Rom. 8:28)

Every event has a purpose. Our joys remind us of God's greatness, and our losses remind us of our dependency on Him. The Lord uses life's difficulties to cultivate maturity within us and to conform us to the image of Christ:

> For those whom He foreknew, He also predestined to become conformed to the image of His Son. (v. 29)

47

Barnabas, Saul, and the others knew that the adventure of following God often meant taking leaps of faith into unknown territory. They knew that being conformed to Christ's image meant at times giving up their own plans and their own rights. So, Barnabas and Paul obediently responded in faith:

> So, being sent out by the Holy Spirit, they went down to Seleucia and from there they sailed to Cyprus. (Acts 13:4)

God had changed these men's lives, and now He was changing their plans! He called them to follow His directives in order to achieve His specific purposes.

## Undergoing Transformation

We begin like caterpillars—sluggishly inching forward on a tree branch, stopping once in a while to nibble on a leaf, then slowly moving forward again. In our caterpillar state, we have no idea that another world awaits us. But then God envelops us with a cocoon of love, and when we awaken, we discover that we have become new, glorious creatures. We're transformed! But we can't experience all God has to offer us until we unfurl our wings in a riot of color and take that first invigorating flight into the great unknown.

Paul referred to this extraordinary transformation in Romans 12:2:

> And do not be conformed to this world, but be transformed by the renewing of your mind, so that you may prove what the will of God is, that which is good and acceptable and perfect.

Note that we're not transformed so we can follow any path we want! We're transformed so that we may follow the path that God has established for us—that of His good, acceptable, and perfect will.

Not only do we *undergo* a radical change when we establish a relationship with Christ, we also should *cause* a radical change. We're His messengers, chosen to take the Gospel to the lost. Instead of simply sighing and accepting the values and lifestyle that the world hands us, we need to be mature, power-filled, and faithful agents of change in our world. Harry Emerson Fosdick wrote:

> Christians are supposed not merely to endure change,

nor even to profit by it, but to *cause* it.[2] (emphasis added)

Isn't it interesting how God uses the most difficult and traumatic experiences of our lives to make us more Christlike? When we fumble and fail, we grow gentle, meek, and humble. We become teachable. We seek God's will through prayer. We read His Word. We're also forced to admit that we're not perfect. We don't have all the answers, and we don't always make the right decisions. We often don't know what to do next. And we realize how dependent we are upon God for every breath and every step.

## Undergoing God's Discipline and Pruning

Christ represents the true Vine, and we are the branches that abide in Him (John 15:1–2). When we grow lackluster or unfruitful due to sin, God disciplines us so that we may again bear fruit. King David understood the negative changes and consequences that can happen in a person's life due to sin. Years after he committed adultery with Bathsheba and ordered the murder of her husband, Uriah, David finally cried out to God for mercy. He implored God:

> Create in me a clean heart, O God,
> And renew a steadfast spirit within me.
> Do not cast me away from your presence
> And do not take Your Holy Spirit from me.
> Restore to me the joy of Your salvation
> And sustain me with a willing spirit.
> Then I will teach transgressors Your ways,
> And sinners will be converted to You.
> (Ps. 51:10–13)[3]

God restored David, but the king experienced severe discipline as a result of his sin. Yet, even when we are faithfully following Him, the Father brings change into our lives so that we will depend upon Him. He prunes our branches so that we may bring forth fruit

---

2. Harry Emerson Fosdick, accessed on October 24, 2002, available at http://www.brainyquote.com.

3. The subheading of Psalm 51 reads, "A Contrite Sinner's Prayer for Pardon" (NASB). The superscription reads, "For the choir director. A Psalm of David, when Nathan the prophet came to him, after he had gone in to Bathsheba."

more abundantly. He teaches us to trust Him and to accept the work He wants to do in us.

Paul and Barnabas experienced God's pruning. They had certain goals for their ministry, but God, the great Change Agent, had other ideas! He sent them out. He reshaped their lives. He called them to a new obedience that challenged their faith and left them asking, "Why?"

As the creative, loving Potter, God had a plan for His clay. He shaped Paul and Barnabas into vessels to be used for His purposes.

## God Is in Control of Change

The prophet Isaiah vividly illustrated this metaphor of God as the Potter and His people as the clay. Isaiah wrote:

> "Woe to the one who quarrels with his Maker—
> An earthenware vessel among the vessels of earth!
> Will the clay say to the potter, 'What are you doing?'
> Or the thing you are making say, 'He has no hands'?"
> (45:9)

He also wrote:

> But now, O Lord, You are our Father,
> We are the clay, and You our potter;
> And all of us are the work of Your hand. (64:8)

God conforms us, shapes us, and molds us to make us more obedient worshipers of Him. One author noted:

> The thorough acquaintance of the potter with both the clay and the vessel that he made from it is used to illustrate God's knowledge of humanity. The power of the potter in molding the clay is used to illustrate the absolute power of God in molding the destinies of men (Rom 9:21). To place one's self as clay in the hands of God, as the potter, is a striking figure of complete trust and surrender (Isa. 64:8).[4]

Have you ever thought about change as a *gift*? Believe it or not, God offers change as a gift to His children—the ones He loves,

---

4. Merrill F. Unger, *The New Unger's Bible Dictionary*, rev. ed., ed. R. K. Harrison (Chicago, Ill.: Moody Press, 1988), see "potter" under the heading "handicrafts."

the ones He created in His own image, the ones for whom His only beloved Son died. Instead of tossing us aside as ugly, gray, good-for-nothing lumps of clay, God lovingly picked us up and made unique and beautiful vessels out of us. Jesus said:

> "If you then, being evil, know how to give good gifts to your children, how much more will your Father who is in heaven give what is good to those who ask Him!" (Matt. 7:11)

God gives good gifts. He has His glory and our best interests at heart. Best of all, no matter what circumstances we face, no matter what occurs in our lives, God never changes! He promises in the book of Malachi:

> "For I, the Lord, do not change . . . Return to Me, and I will return to you," says the Lord of hosts. (Mal. 3:6a, 7b)

Our Father's love, His power, His knowledge, and His plan are perfect. He is the same yesterday, today, and forever! When the winds of change blow and your ship is tossed about on stormy seas, call out to the One who made you, the One who loves you. He promises to be your anchor in times of trouble.

 *Living Insights*

The philosopher Heraclitus once said, "There is nothing permanent except change."[5] Serendipities, changes, and surprises add to the fun and adventure of living a life of faith.

What changes have you been challenged to make in your life as a result of your adventure with God?

_____

_____

_____

_____

5. Heraclitus, at http://www.heartquotes.net/Change.html, accessed on October 24, 2002.

What changes do you expect to occur in the next year regarding your spiritual life, family, marriage, church, school, and so on?

_____

_____

_____

_____

How do you plan to face these changes? How can you start to prepare spiritually for the *unexpected*?

_____

_____

_____

_____

How has God used unexpected events or circumstances in the past to help you grow in your faith?

_____

_____

_____

_____

Have you ever experienced God's pruning so that you would bear more fruit? If so, what happened?

_____

_____

_____

_____

We challenge you to make this year a true adventure with God. Launch out courageously into the great unknown and make a difference for His kingdom. And remember: our great God never changes!

# BOOKS FOR
# PROBING FURTHER

We hope that you've been encouraged in your adventure with God. We pray that you were challenged to live a life of solid faith and breathless expectation, trusting God to lead you along your serendipitous journey. These additional resources will help you continue on your adventurous path. You'll be challenged to grow and mature in your faith as you dig into these books and discover the treasures they contain. These resources will help you find the courage and faith you need to grab God's hand and take that leap into the great unknown!

Blackaby, Henry T. and Claude V. King. *Experiencing God: How to Live the Full Adventure of Knowing and Doing the Will of God.* New York, N.Y.: Broadman and Holman, 1998.

Bonhoeffer, Dietrich. *The Cost of Discipleship.* New York, N.Y.: Simon and Schuster, 2001.

Bright, Bill. *First Love: Renewing Your Passion for God.* Orlando, Fla.: New Life Publications, 2002.

Eldredge, John. *Wild at Heart.* Nashville, Tenn.: Thomas Nelson Publishers, 2001.

Lewis, Robert with Rob Wilkins. *The Church of Irresistible Influence.* Grand Rapids, Mich.: Zondervan Publishing House, 2001.

Mabery-Foster, Lucy. *Women and the Church: Reaching, Teaching, and Developing Women for Christ.* Nashville, Tenn.: Word Publishing, 1999.

McManus, Erwin Raphael. *Seizing Your Divine Moment: Dare to Live a Life of Adventure.* Nashville, Tenn.: Thomas Nelson Publishers, 2002.

Patterson, Ben. *Deepening Your Conversation with God: Learning to Love to Pray.* Minneapolis, Minn.: Bethany House Publishers, 2001.

Schreiner, Thomas R. *Paul: Apostle of God's Glory in Christ.* Downers Grove, Ill.: InterVarsity Press, 2001.

Shibley, David, and Ron Luce. *The Missions Addiction: Capturing God's Passion for the World*. Lake Mary, Fla.: Charisma House Publishers, 2001.

Stott, John. *The Message of Acts: The Spirit, the Church, and the World*. Downers Grove, Ill.: InterVarsity Press, 1994.

Wilkinson, Bruce. *Secrets of the Vine: Breaking through to Abundance*. Portland, Ore.: Multnomah Publishing Inc., 2001.

Yancey, Philip. *Church: Why Bother?* Grand Rapids, Mich.: Zondervan Publishing House, 1998.

————. *What's So Amazing About Grace?* Grand Rapids, Mich.: Zondervan Publishing House, 1997.

Some of the books listed may be out of print and available only through a library. For those currently available, please contact your local Christian bookstore. Books by Charles R. Swindoll and many books by other authors may be obtained through the Insight for Living Resource Center.

Insight for Living also has Bible study guides available on many books of the Bible as well as on a variety of topics, Bible characters, and contemporary issues. For more information, see the ordering instructions that follow and contact the office that serves you.

# NOTES

# NOTES

# NOTES

# ORDERING INFORMATION

## ADVENTURING WITH GOD:
## FOLLOWING IN THE APOSTLES' FOOTSTEPS

If you would like to order additional Bible study guides, purchase the audio series that accompanies this guide, or request our product catalogs, please contact the office that serves you.

**United States and International locations:**
Insight for Living
Post Office Box 269000
Plano, TX 75026-9000

1-800-772-8888, 24 hours a day, seven days a week (U.S. contacts)
International constituents may contact the U.S. office through mail queries.

**Canada:**
Insight for Living Ministries
Post Office Box 2510
Vancouver, BC V6B 3W7

1-800-663-7639, 24 hours a day, seven days a week
info@insightcanada.org

**Australia:**
Insight for Living, Inc.
20 Albert Street
Blackburn, VIC 3130, Australia

Toll-free 1800 772 888 or (03) 9877-4277, 9:00 A.M. to 5:00 P.M., Monday to Friday
iflaus@insight.org

**Internet:**
www.insight.org

### Bible Study Guide Subscription Program

Bible study guide subscriptions are available. Please call or write the office nearest you to find out how you can receive our Bible study guides on a regular basis.